Developing
Grade 2 Reading Fluency

Written by
Trisha Callella

Editor: Teri L. Applebaum
Illustrator: Ann Iosa
Cover Illustrator: Chris Ellithorpe
Designer: Mary Gagné
Cover Designer: Mary Gagné
Art Director: Tom Cochrane
Project Director: Carolea Williams

Table of Contents

Fluency Activities and Strategies

Intervention Activities and Strategies

Introduction

Learning to read is a systematic, learned process. Once children can read individual words, they need to learn to put those words together to form sentences. Then, children must learn to read those sentences fluently to comprehend not only the meaning of each word but also the meaning of an entire sentence. Children's reading fluency develops as they learn to break sentences into phrases and to "chunk" words together into phrases as they read. As children read sentences in phrases, they develop better comprehension of each sentence's meaning.

Use the lessons in *Developing Reading Fluency* to meet district, state, and national reading standards as you teach children how to develop reading fluency. The first five sections are arranged sequentially to help you implement fluency modeling, fluency practice by children, and then children's application of fluency strategies. Use the activities to help children build upon the skills they learned in the previous section. The final section of the book contains additional instruction to provide intervention for children having difficulties. The book features the following strategies to improve children's reading fluency:

- **Interactive Read-Alouds:** Use modeled and choral reading with the whole class or small groups to increase children's listening comprehension and to give them experience with rereading short rhymed phrases.
- **Cheers and Chants:** Model how to correctly read text, and teach children to echo your phrasing and fluency. These activities use guided practice and choral reading with the whole class or small groups.
- **Read-Arounds:** Help children learn high-frequency and content words and practice reading text in phrases as they work in small groups.
- **Plays for Two:** Use these simple scripts to have children practice with a partner repeated oral reading strategies as they develop phrasing and fluency.
- **Reader's Theater:** Have children work in groups of four to practice rereading a script until they can fluently read their part in front of an audience. Use the performances as a culminating activity to have children apply all the reading strategies they have learned.
- **Intervention Instruction:** Use these activities with individuals or small groups to intervene with children who still struggle with reading fluency. These activities enable children to identify and practice expression, intonation, and the natural flow of fluency.

The activities in this book provide children with a variety of reading experiences. The themes and genres included in each section will motivate children to not only read the text but to read with expression, intonation, and a natural flow. Children will build enthusiasm and confidence as they begin to increase their comprehension and as they successfully apply reading strategies to their everyday reading!

Reading fluency is the ability to read with expression, intonation, and a natural flow that sounds like talking. Fluency is not the speed at which one reads. That is the reading rate. A fluent reader does read quickly; however, he or she also focuses on phrased units of meaning. A child may read quickly but may not necessarily be fluent. Children who read too quickly often skip over punctuation. This inhibits comprehension because punctuation helps convey meaning. Fluent readers have developed automaticity. This means that they have a solid bank of sight words on which they can rely and that are automatic. Fluent readers can then focus their reading on understanding the message rather than decoding the text. Reading is decoding with comprehension. Fluent readers do both. They read without thinking about how they are reading, and they understand what they are reading.

What does a child who lacks fluency sound like?
A child who lacks fluency may sound choppy, robotic, or speedy.

How does repeated oral reading increase fluency?
Research shows that children increase their fluency when they read and reread the same passage aloud several times. The support that teachers give children during oral reading by modeling the text and providing guidance and feedback enhances their fluency development. Using this strategy, children gradually become better readers and their word recognition, speed, accuracy, and fluency all increase as a result. Their comprehension also improves because they are bridging the gap between reading for word recognition and reading for meaning.

Why should I worry about fluency when children are only emergent readers?
Bad habits can be hard to break. Research has found that poor reading habits stand in the way of children becoming fluent readers. Research has also found that children can and do become fluent even as emergent readers. Those emergent, fluent readers carry that fluency onto more difficult text and therefore have a higher level of comprehension. Fluency activities should be incorporated into every classroom, beginning in kindergarten with modeled reading, shared reading, guided reading, and independent reading.

How do fluency and phrasing work together?
Phrasing is the link between decoding the meaning of the text and reading the text fluently. Phrasing is the way that a reader groups the words. A lack of phrasing results in staccato reading, "word calling," and decoding. A fluent reader reads quickly in phrased chunks that are meaningful. Read the information on page 5 to learn more about phrasing.

Phrasing

A child who reads in phrases reads words in meaningful groups. Phrasing helps a child understand that the text carries meaning. A phrase is a group of words that the reader says together and reads together. The way the words are grouped affects the meaning. This is why phrasing affects reading comprehension.

What does phrasing sound like?

Consider how the same sentence can have different meanings depending on the way the words are grouped, or phrased. It clearly affects the comprehension of what is read. For example:

Patti Lee is my best friend.

Patti, Lee is my best friend.

Who is the best friend? It depends on how the sentence is read. In this example, punctuation also affects phrasing.

What causes incorrect phrasing?

A child may read with incorrect phrasing for a number of reasons. First of all, many children in second grade still rely too much on phonics. This leads to a dependency on decoding. When children focus on decoding, they neglect the message. They turn into expert "word callers." Incorrect phrasing can also result from a lack of attention to punctuation. Some children ignore punctuation altogether, which will result in incorrect phrasing, will affect their fluency, and will hurt their comprehension.

What can I do to teach and improve phrasing?

1. Use the activities in this book. They are all researched, teacher-tested, and student-approved, and they will help children experience reading fluency success.
2. Stop pointing to each word during shared reading because that reinforces word-by-word reading. Once children can point and read with one-to-one correspondence, begin shared reading with a finger sweep under phrases. (Finger sweeps look like a stretched out "u.") This strategy models and reinforces phrasing.
3. Read and reread.
4. Model. Model. Model.
5. Echo read.
6. Make flash cards of common phrases to help children train their eyes to see words in groups rather than as individual words.
7. Tape-record children as they read. Let them listen to improvements they make in phrasing and intonation.

How to Use This Book

The activities in this book provide fun and easy strategies that will help children develop reading fluency. Getting started is simple.

- Use the Stages of Fluency Development chart on page 7 to assess the children's ability. Take notes as children read aloud, and then refer to the chart to see at what stage of fluency development they are. Use this information to create a plan of action and to decide on which skills the whole class, groups of children, and individuals need to focus.
- Use the Fantastic Five Format on page 8 with the whole class, small groups, or individuals. This format provides a guideline for developing reading fluency that will work with any genre. Copy the reproducible, and use it as a "cheat sheet" when you give guided instruction. You will find the format effective in helping you with modeling, teaching, guiding, and transferring phrased and fluent reading to independent reading.
- Refer to the Teacher Tips on page 9 before you begin using the activities in this book. These tips include helpful information that will assist you as you teach all the children in your classroom to read fluently and, as a result, improve their comprehension of text.

Fluency Activities and Strategies

The first five sections of this book have been sequentially arranged for you to first model fluency, then have children practice fluency, and finally have them independently apply their newly learned skills. Each section has an introductory page to help you get started. It includes

- an explanation of how the activities in that section relate to fluency development
- the strategies children will use to complete the activities
- a materials list
- step-by-step directions for preparing and presenting the activities
- an idea for how to extend the activities

Each section opener is followed by a set of fun reproducible reading materials that are designed to excite and motivate children about developing reading fluency. Within each section, the readability of the reproducibles increases in difficulty to provide appropriate reading material for second graders who read at different levels.

Intervention Activities and Strategies

The last section of the book provides additional instruction and practice to help children who have difficulty with reading fluency. This section contains several activities designed for use with individuals or small groups. Each activity has its own page of directions that lists strategies, an objective, materials, and step-by-step directions. Reassess children often to determine their reading fluency level and their need for intervention.

Stages of Fluency Development

Stage	What You Observe	What to Teach for Fluency
1	• many miscues • too much emphasis on meaning • storytelling based on pictures • sounds fluent but not reading what is written down • playing "teacher" while reading	• print carries the meaning
2	• tries to match what he or she says with what is written on the page • one-to-one correspondence • finger pointing and "voice pointing" • staccato reading, robotic reading	• phrasing and fluency • focus on meaning • read like talking • high-frequency words • purpose of punctuation
3	• focuses on the meaning of print • may use bookmarks • focuses more on print than picture • no longer voice points • laughs, giggles, or comments while reading	• phrasing and fluency • focus on what makes sense and looks right • purpose of punctuation • proper expression and intonation
4	• reads books with more print than pictures • wants to talk about what he or she read • reads like talking with phrasing • reads punctuation with expression • laughs, giggles, or comments while reading	• shades of meaning • making connections

Fantastic Five Format

Step 1

Modeled Fluency

Model reading with fluency so that children understand the text and what they are supposed to learn.

Step 2

Echo Reading

Read one part. Have children repeat the same part.

Step 3

Choral Reading

Read together. This prepares children to take over the task of reading.

Step 4

Independent Fluency

Have children read to you.

Step 5

Reverse Echo Reading

Have children read to you, and then repeat their phrasing, expression, and fluency. Children have now taken over the task of reading.

Developing Reading Fluency • Gr. 2 © 2003 Creative Teaching Press

1. Be aware of how you arrange rhymes, stories, and poems in a pocket chart. Often, teachers put each line in a separate pocket. When teachers do this, children do not recognize phrases and they begin to think that sentences always end on the right. (That is one reason why children often put a period at the end of every line in their writing journals.) Instead, cut the sentences or rhymes into meaningful phrased chunks so that children see and read what you model and teach.

2. If you use guided reading in your classroom, incorporate time for children to reread familiar books. Keep guided reading books that were once used for instructional purposes in bins that are color-coded to represent different ability levels. Have each child choose two books to reread as warm-ups every time you meet. This helps children put phrasing and fluency instruction into practice. Remember, use books that are appropriate to children's independent-reading level (books that can be read with 95 percent accuracy).

3. Write a daily Morning Message that follows a predictable format. Follow the Fantastic Five Format on page 8 to develop phrasing and fluency and improve reading comprehension.

4. Have a Friend of the Day tell you three things about himself or herself. Model for the class how to write the child's information in phrases on a piece of white construction paper. Read it in phrases and choral read it for fluency. Reread all of the information about previous Friends of the Day prior to writing about the new Friend. Bind the pages together into a class book, and have children read it independently or take it home to share with their family.

5. Once a child matches speech to print, do not allow him or her to point when reading. It is important to train children's eyes to look at words in groups rather than at one word at a time. While reading aloud, fluent readers look at many words ahead of what they read.

6. If children must use bookmarks to track words as they read, have them hold the bookmark just above the line of print they are reading rather than just under the line. When children use a bookmark under a line of print, the bookmark blocks the next line. This keeps children from reading fluently because they cannot see the ending punctuation. Try it—you will find that you cannot read fluently with a bookmark under the line you read. You will be amazed how this small change affects children's reading.

Learn to read with fluency!

Interactive Read-Alouds

Comprehension begins at the listening stage. Children understand what they hear before they understand what they read. That is why research supports reading aloud to children books and stories that are above their reading level. Reading aloud builds vocabulary, models thinking aloud, and models phrasing and fluency. This activity takes reading aloud a step further by including rhymed phrases that children will then use to apply the repeated oral reading strategy. The structure of this activity will keep children actively listening.

Strategies: repeated oral reading, modeled fluency, choral reading, active listening

Materials
- overhead projector/ transparencies or chart paper (optional)

Directions

1. Choose one story, and make one copy of the reproducible. Copy a class set of the corresponding rhymed phrases. Or, as an option, make an overhead transparency of the reproducible or write the rhymed phrases on the board or chart paper.

2. NOTE: Do not photocopy the story for children. This activity is designed to build children's listening comprehension. They need to hear phrasing and fluency modeled by you in order to replicate it in their own reading.

3. Give each child a copy of the rhymed phrases, or display the phrases so all the children can see them. Read aloud the phrases, and have children practice reading them. Tell children that you will read aloud a story and that they will read aloud the rhymed phrases each time you point to them. (Point to the class each time you see an asterisk in the story.)

4. For "The Shopping Trip" on page 17, invite the class to fill in the blank at the end of the story. For "Wonderful Whales" on page 19, gather a plastic zippered bag, three or four rocks, a tub that is 2/3 full of water, a spoon, and shortening for each small group of children. Invite children to perform the experiment in the story as you read aloud the story. Write the limerick at the bottom of the story on chart paper or the board so all children can read it.

5. Read aloud the story. Model good phrasing, intonation, and fluency.

6. Throughout the story, stop at each asterisk, point to the children, and have them read the rhymed phrases, with increased fluency each time.

Extension

Many of the rhymed phrases lend themselves to movements. Make up silly movements that children can do as they read their part. This will maximize active listening. Try movements such as clicking tongues, clapping, stomping feet, moving hands like waves in the ocean, moving hands up together and then parting them in opposite ways, nodding heads, hopping, turning around, and cross-lateral movements.

Spotty's Adventure

Have you ever had a pet rabbit? What do you know about rabbits? I am sure you know that they are small, furry, and cute. We all know that they move by hopping and they love carrots, but what do rabbits like to do all day?

I want you to picture a black and white rabbit with black ears, a white face, and a black spot near his mouth. That's Spotty! Guess how he got his name. That's right, because of the black spot on his face. He's one crazy rabbit! *

Spotty is a pet rabbit who has an unusual life. He doesn't live in a burrow in the ground. Instead, he lives in an office. He gets to run around all day. * He has a cage he can go into when he needs to visit his litter box or just take a little nap. However, he really likes to run around the office most of the day. *

Spotty loves people! If you visited the office, he would greet you at the door and run around your feet! Of course, he would be thinking, "Pick me up, please!" Sometimes, he gets to play in the yard when other animals are not around. He runs so fast! He likes to nibble on the grass, hop into the air, and lay flat on his belly. *

Most of all, Spotty likes playing with people. You see, he thinks people are just big rabbits! I know it sounds crazy, but it's true. He follows people around in the office all the time! His favorite thing to do, in fact, is to hop up onto people's laps while they are working on their computers. Can you picture it? * It's a problem sometimes, since he then jumps onto their desks. What do you think Spotty accidentally does? You guessed it. He accidentally erases some of the work the people are doing on their computers. They don't mind since they were smart and saved their work along the way. It always makes them laugh and smile. Can you picture it? *

One day, Spotty decided to go play outside. He was doing his usual "happy hops" when a frog jumped out of the bushes. Spotty had not ever seen a frog before. He froze! He didn't know what to do. You won't believe what that silly rabbit did! He started running around the frog in circles! * It seemed like Spotty was trying to make friends with the frog the way he did with the people in the office. The people laughed so hard! Spotty had to be the friendliest bunny around!

Just then, as Spotty was circling the frog for the third time, the frog jumped up. It landed right on Spotty! What a shock! Spotty ran right back into the office, jumped on his box, and hid in his cage. The frog just sat there. It was hard to tell which animal was more scared!

Everybody went back inside to see what Spotty was doing. Spotty slowly came out and waited for someone to pick him up. Five minutes later, he was fast asleep in someone's arms. That little adventure truly wore him out! Everyone smiled and someone said, "I bet he's dreaming about running in the sun without any frogs around!" *

Interactive Read-Alouds

Spotty's Adventure
Rhymed Phrases

I can picture Spotty playing in the sun.

I can picture Spotty having so much fun.

Run Spotty, run Spotty, run in the sun!

Spotty's Adventure
Rhymed Phrases

I can picture Spotty playing in the sun.

I can picture Spotty having so much fun.

Run Spotty, run Spotty, run in the sun!

Developing Reading Fluency • Gr. 2 © 2003 Creative Teaching Press

The Day Everything Was Upside Down — Theme: fantasy

I think it all started when I made one tiny wish. Do you want to know what it was? I wished that I could walk upside down. Now, you might think that sounds a little crazy. However, I wanted to see the world from a different angle. I think that's how the whole crazy day started, but I don't know why my silly wish really came true!

Yesterday morning, * Yes, that's right! Everything was upside down! Not just a lamp or a clock. EVERYTHING was upside down! I woke up and got out of bed headfirst instead of feet-first. Oh, my! I thought I had to be dreaming. So I looked around my room. You will never believe what I saw! *

My doll was on the ceiling, but that was really the floor. Oh, how very confusing it all was. I couldn't believe my eyes! I immediately thought that someone had done something to my room. Naturally, I went out into my hallway to prove that I was still waking up and that every-thing was the same as usual. Guess what? * That's right. The lamp that usually hangs from my hallway ceiling was standing on my hallway floor! My dog walked by me on the ceiling! What was I going to do?

I closed my eyes and made a new wish. I said, "I wish that the world would be normal again." I opened my eyes and * Did my house turn upside down because of me? How could that be? No, that would be impossible! I'm only eight years old. I don't have any special powers. I'm an ordinary second-grade kid. How could one silly wish change the world?

I thought about what I could do. Then I realized that it had to be only my home. It couldn't really be the world. So . . . I walked outside. (Yes, I was still in my pajamas.) * "Oh, no!" I thought. This can't be happening. Surely, I'm still asleep and this is just a wild dream. The cars were driving in the sky! The birds were walking on the ground! People were walking down the street in midair—upside down!

This just couldn't be! I decided there was only one thing I could do—go back to bed. I laid down in my bed and closed my eyes. I tried counting sheep, but I couldn't fall asleep. Was I already asleep? I was so confused, so I opened up one eye to take a little peek and . . . *

I just had to close my eyes as tightly as possible after that. I made a new wish. I said, "I wish I may, I wish I might, undo the wish I made last night." Then, I decided I really had to go back to sleep for the wish to work. So . . . I went to sleep. Guess what I saw when I woke up? Everything was back to normal! Hooray! Just another ordinary day!

The Day Everything Was Upside Down
Rhymed Phrases

I woke up in the morning.

Everything was upside down!

I peeked outside my window.

It was the same way all over town!

The Day Everything Was Upside Down
Rhymed Phrases

I woke up in the morning.

Everything was upside down!

I peeked outside my window.

It was the same way all over town!

Developing Reading Fluency • Gr. 2 © 2003 Creative Teaching Press

The Storm

I was so scared! It was my first sleepover at a friend's house. It was a good thing I brought my favorite teddy bear with me. Three of us were going to spend the night at our friend's house. I couldn't believe that my dad agreed to let me go! I've been asking for two years, and he always said "no." He was worried something would happen and he wouldn't be there to help. Well, I did wish he was there that night!

At first, we were all having fun. We ate hot dogs, played cards, and watched a movie. So far, I had been having a great time. We were laughing so hard! Then, our friend's mom came in and told us it was time to go to bed. We all got ready and climbed into our sleeping bags. Just as we were settling in for a good night's rest, we heard ✳

I have to admit that I was the first person who jumped. I was scared! I wanted to go home right away! I knew it was raining outside, but I didn't know the weather was going to get so stormy. Suddenly, ✳ I tried to remember what I learned about stormy weather in school to calm me down. My teacher told me it was just a sign of nature and that we did not need to be afraid. The rain came down when the clouds couldn't hold any more water droplets. My thinking was interrupted by ✳

Now let me see (I said to myself). It's just a storm. Nothing to be afraid of. I returned to what I had learned. It was helping to calm me down. Oh, that's right. A thunderstorm begins when warm and damp air rises quickly. The warm air bumps into the cooler air that is falling to the ground. Then, more damp air will rise and condense. When that happens, the clouds grow big and tall and turn into storm clouds. My thoughts were interrupted by ✳

At that instant, I hugged my teddy bear a little bit tighter. All I could think about was calling my dad to ask him to pick me up. I was scared even though I was with my friends in a safe house. The lightning and thunder were getting closer together. We were all so quiet. Just then, our friend's mom came into the room to check on us. She could see that we were all scared. She told us not to worry. It was just a storm. We told her that the thunder sounded scary. She reminded us that the thunder we hear is the sound that lightning makes when it goes through the air. We see the lightning before we hear the thunder because light travels faster than sound. Just then we heard ✳

Suddenly, the phone rang. It was my dad calling to see how I was doing. He must have been scared without me. I told him what I learned about thunder and lightning. I told him not to be scared. I also told him that I loved him. Right after I hung up the phone, I heard ✳

The Storm
Rhymed Phrases

Roar, crash, boom! Roar, crash, boom!

I see lightning in the sky go z-o-o-m!

Roar, crash, boom! Roar, crash, boom!

Now I hear thunder outside my room!

- -

The Storm
Rhymed Phrases

Roar, crash, boom! Roar, crash, boom!

I see lightning in the sky go z-o-o-m!

Roar, crash, boom! Roar, crash, boom!

Now I hear thunder outside my room!

Developing Reading Fluency • Gr. 2 © 2003 Creative Teaching Press

The Shopping Trip

Wow! What a birthday! I got so many nice things from my friends and family. The new jacket is the best. I can't wait to wear it when we go camping! I have to remember to write my thank-you cards this weekend. Mom said that after I write my thank-you cards we can go to the bank to deposit the money I received. I have a better idea! *

I think that I should be able to spend at least some of the money. Now, I know that I have to save for college. After all, Harvard is an expensive university. However, I am an eight-year-old kid now. I have plenty of time to save for college. I think I should be able to go shopping with a little bit of my money. What do you think? *

Perhaps if I write really good thank-you cards my mom will change her mind. I'll give it a try. I think I'll make a list of the reasons why I should be able to spend a little bit of the money on a shopping trip. I'll show the list to my parents. Who knows? Maybe I'll be able to persuade them to change their minds just a little bit. I don't want to spend it all, just a few dollars on a neat new toy.

(three days later)

"Mom! Dad! I finished my thank-you cards. I wrote one to every person who gave me a present or a card. I also wrote a little list to share with you. I think I should be able to spend a few dollars of my birthday money and save the rest for college. Here's my list of reasons why I think that's a fair idea." In my mind I was busy thinking . . . *

(after reading the list)

"You have some very good points," said my mom. "I think we can compromise. You can spend twenty dollars on anything you want at the toy store. The rest will go into your college account. That seems fair to me. Do you agree?" "Thanks, Mom! I may not even spend that much! I just want to pick out a little something." Then my mom surprised me by saying, "Let's go shopping!" All I could think of was . . . *

(in the toy store)

"Mom, can we go down the game aisle? I saw a game on TV that looked like fun." * "Oh, wait a minute. Let's look down this aisle first. I might want a new paint set instead. Oh, that will cost too much. I know our deal was twenty dollars and that's enough for me. No paint set. Let's go check out those games!" * "There it is! That's the game! It's on sale for only $9.99! What a deal! Can I buy Mystery Match, Mom?" "Sure, this is your shopping spree," she said. On the way to the cash register I was thinking * Then, my mom said, "What will you do with the money you have left over?" Of course, I said, "_____."

Developing Reading Fluency • Gr. 2 © 2003 Creative Teaching Press

Interactive Read-Alouds

The Shopping Trip
Rhymed Phrases

Ka-ching, ka-ching,

I want to buy something!

Mom says money belongs in a savings account.

Dad says I should save any amount.

But, ka-ching, ka-ching,

I want to buy something!

Developing Reading Fluency • Gr. 2 © 2003 Creative Teaching Press

Wonderful Whales

Theme: whales are mammals (science experiment tie-in)

Thank you for inviting me to your class today! As you know, I am a whale expert. I have studied whales for many years. I now work at the ABC Aquarium where I give tours to classes just like yours. I love teaching children about the whales and their habitats. Are you ready to learn about whales? First of all, we're going to play a little game. Every time I point to you, you will say this limerick: ✱ When we are finished learning about whales, we will do a quick and easy experiment to learn about how blubber works. ✱

First of all, let's see what you know about whales. You all know they are living things because they breathe, grow, and need water. How do they breathe? Do they have gills like the fish that they share the ocean with? ✱ You are so clever! You are absolutely right. Whales have lungs that help them breathe and they exhale through the blowhole on the top of their head.

Where do whales live? Do they live in rivers, lakes, or seas? How do they dive so deep into the water? ✱ Look at how much you already know about whales! You are amazing! What do whales have to keep them warm that we do not have, although we are also mammals? ✱ That's right! Whales have layers of blubber under their skin that helps to keep them warm. Let's learn a little about how that works by doing a simple experiment.

We are going to work in groups of four. Each group will have a plastic zippered bag of three or four rocks, a tub that is about 2/3 full of water, a spoon, and some shortening. Now, we all know that a whale is very large and heavy. So the rocks represent the whale's muscles, bones, and organs. Do you all have your "whales" ready? Put them in the bag. Squeeze almost all of the air out of the bag and close the bag. Tell me what you know about whales. ✱ Terrific! Let's put our whales in the water and see what happens. (*Wait while children do this.*) Why do you think our whales sank? (*Listen to responses.*) What do our whales need? (*Wait for them to say "blubber."*) Now, what do you think the shortening will represent? (*Listen to responses.*) You're right—the blubber! Let's add some blubber. About two or three spoonfuls will do. (*Tell children to squeeze almost all of the air out of the bag and close it.*) What happened? (*Listen to responses.*) Why is it important for a whale to have blubber? (*Listen to responses.*)

Now that you understand how blubber works, you are ready to teach your family tonight what you learned about whales. What will you say to them? ✱ Outstanding! Here's one more limerick for you to teach them. Let's practice it together.

> Whales are mammals you'll agree.
> They have lungs to breathe just like me.
> Their blubber helps them float
> Along the surface like a boat,
> While it keeps them warm in the ice-cold sea.

Developing Reading Fluency • Gr. 2 © 2003 Creative Teaching Press

Interactive Read-Alouds

Wonderful Whales
Rhymed Phrases

Whales are mammals you see.
They're warm-blooded like you and me.
They breathe air to survive.
Their tail fluke moves up and down to help them dive.
And their blubber helps them float in the sea.

Wonderful Whales
Rhymed Phrases

Whales are mammals you see.
They're warm-blooded like you and me.
They breathe air to survive.
Their tail fluke moves up and down to help them dive.
And their blubber helps them float in the sea.

Developing Reading Fluency • Gr. 2 © 2003 Creative Teaching Press

Cheers and Chants

An important part of learning to read is motivation and excitement. Through shared reading, you share that excitement with the class. You create a positive learning environment while reinforcing phrasing and fluency in reading, which are directly related to reading comprehension. Each Cheers and Chants rhyme is designed for the whole class or small groups.

Strategies: repeated oral reading, modeled reading, echo reading, choral reading

Materials

• chart paper, sentence strips/pocket chart, or overhead transparency/ projector

Directions

1. Choose a cheer or chant for the class to read. Decide how you want to present it to the class. (Each child needs to be able to see the text.) You can write it on chart paper, write it on sentence strips to place in a pocket chart, make a copy for each child, or make and display an overhead transparency.

2. Read aloud the cheer or chant several times. This will introduce children to the text and will model correct phrasing, intonation, and fluency. For "Parts of Plants" on page 25, read aloud the chant to model fluency, then read it aloud using choral reading, and, finally, invite children to apply fluency by reading alternating lines.

3. Invite children to echo read or choral read the text.

4. To extend this activity, make copies of the reproducibles on construction paper or tagboard, and laminate them. Invite children to take home a cheer or chant to practice reading with their family.

Extension

Follow the Fantastic Five Format (see page 8) to incorporate modeled fluency, guided fluency, and independent fluency practice.

Step 1: **Modeled Fluency**—Display the chant or cheer. Read it as the class follows along.
Step 2: **Echo Reading**—Read one part. Have the class repeat the same part.
Step 3: **Choral Reading**—Read together. This prepares children to take over the task of reading.
Step 4: **Independent Fluency**—Have children read to you.
Step 5: **Reverse Echo Reading**—Have children read to you, and repeat after them.

Sharing

Theme: character education

This is mine!

That's not yours!

Listen to how silly that sounds!

We can take turns.

You go first!

That's the way sharing goes around!

You share with me.

I'll share with you.

That's the way new friends are found!

Developing Reading Fluency • Gr. 2 © 2003 Creative Teaching Press

Classroom Pledge

Today is a new day.

Today is my fresh start.

I will work hard

And do my part.

I will share materials

And clean up right away.

I will listen to everything

That you have to say!

In everything I do,

I will show respect to you!

Cheers and Chants

Friend of the Week

Theme: celebrations

(can be chanted to the tune of "Someone's in the Kitchen with Dinah")

We have a new friend of the week.

I'm holding his or her name, but you can't peek!

We have a new friend who will share with you

Pictures and facts about what he or she likes to do.

Now let's sing.

Hip, hip, hip, hooray!

Let's meet our new friend right away!

Hip, hip, hip, hooray!

_____'s our friend of the week—HOORAY!

Developing Reading Fluency • Gr. 2 © 2003 Creative Teaching Press

Parts of Plants

Teacher   What's green, needs light, and has strong roots?

Children   Plants are green, need light, and have strong roots.

Teacher   What are the other parts of a plant?

Children   The stem and leaves are part of the plant.

Teacher   Which part helps hold the plant in place?

Children   The roots help hold the plant in place.

Teacher   Which part carries water and minerals to the leaves?

Children   The stem carries water and minerals to the leaves.

Teacher   Which part catches light from the sun to make food for the plant?

Children   The leaves catch light from the sun to make food for the plant.

Teacher   What are the parts of the plant called?

Teacher and Children Echo Response
Roots, a stem, and leaves are on every plant!

Cheers and Chants

Second-Grade Superstars

I'm a second-grade superstar!

I'm a success! I'm going far!

I can read many books that are long.

I learn every time I get something wrong.

I try to study hard for each test.

I focus on always doing my best!

I try to be patient and I share.

I try to be responsible and I care.

I'm a second-grade superstar!

Watch me! I will really go far!

Developing Reading Fluency • Gr. 2 © 2003 Creative Teaching Press

Keep Trying

If at first I cannot do it,

I will try and try again.

It may take a bit more thinking,

So I will try and try again.

No one succeeds by giving up,

So I will try and try again.

If I still cannot figure it out,

I will try and try again.

(can be chanted to the tune of "peanut—peanut butter—JELLY")

Keep on, keep on trying—you did it!

Keep on, keep on trying—you did it!

Cheers and Chants

Happy Birthday!

(can be chanted to the tune of the theme song from "The Addams Family"; include snapping)

Theme: celebrations

Today it is your birthday,

So happy, happy birthday!

It's time to celebrate.

You're another year older today!

This is your day. *(snap, snap)*

We'll shout "hooray." *(snap, snap)*

We wish you fun,

We wish you joy

On your special day! *(snap, snap)*

HAPPY BIRTHDAY!

Developing Reading Fluency • Gr. 2 © 2003 Creative Teaching Press

Ancestors

We all have people in our family

Who are no longer here for us to see.

Your mom had a mom who had a mom, too.

She would be your great-grandma if she were here with you.

Ancestors are part of your family tree.

They are related to you—it's in your history.

To learn about your ancestors all you need to do

Is list the people in your family—it all begins with you!

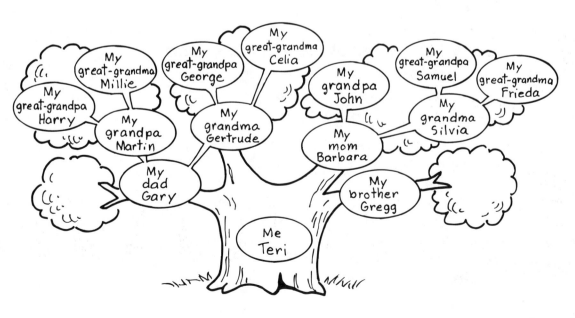

Read-Arounds

According to research, one reason why children do not read with phrasing and fluency is that they do not have a solid base of high-frequency words and sight words, which is required for reading books independently. Research recommends activities that give children practice with frequently used words. This will in turn help with phrasing and fluency because children will not need to slow down to decode as often. The Read-Around cards in this section are already written in phrases (spaces between groups of words), so children can see and better understand how to read words in groups. The Read-Around cards are designed for groups of two to four children. This allows for optimal amounts of practice and active involvement. The phrases on the cards are short and simple to help children focus directly on reading phrases and practicing high-frequency and content words.

Strategies: phrased reading; repeated oral reading; active listening; reading high-frequency, content, and sight words

Materials
- construction paper or tagboard
- scissors
- envelopes

Directions

1. Choose a set of cards (e.g., synonyms, ordinal numbers), and copy the cards on construction paper or tagboard. (Each set of cards is two pages.) Cut apart the cards, and laminate them so that they can be reused throughout the school year. Put the cards in an envelope, and write the title (e.g., *Synonyms*) on the envelope.

2. Give a set of cards to a small group of children so that each child has one to three cards. Review with children the pronunciation and meaning of the bold words on their clue cards so that they are familiar and comfortable with those key words (or preteach the words).

3. Explain that children will play a listening and reading game. Model how the game works and the correct answers with each group the first time children play using a new set of cards. Read aloud each child's cards, and then have children silently read their cards at least five times to build fluency. Discuss each question and corresponding answer so children can concentrate more on reading fluently than on determining the answer to the question as they play.

4. Tell the group that the child who has the clue card that says *I have the first card* will begin the game by reading aloud his or her card. After the first card is read aloud, have the child with the answer to the clue read aloud his or her card. Tell children to continue until they get back to the first card. (The game ends after a child reads *Who has the first card?* and a child answers *I have the first card*.)

5. Encourage children to play the game at least twice. Have them mix up the cards and pass the cards out again so that children read different cards each time.

Extension

Invite children to take home a set of cards. Have them teach their family how to play and practice reading the cards with family members. Encourage families to make additional cards.

Contractions 1 (using 's and 're)

I have   the first card.

Who has the word   that joins **it is**?

I have   the word **it's**.

Who has the word   that joins **that is**?

I have   the word **that's**.

Who has the word   that joins **she is**?

I have   the word **she's**.

Who has the word   that joins **you are**?

I have   the word **you're**.

Who has the word   that joins **they are**?

Developing Reading Fluency • Gr. 2 © 2003 Creative Teaching Press

Read-Arounds

Contractions 1 (using 's and 're)

I have   the word **they're**.

Who has the word   that joins **we are**?

I have   the word **we're**.

Who has the word   that joins **he is**?

I have   the word **he's**.

Who has the word   that joins **what is**?

I have   the word **what's**.

Who has the word   that joins **where is**?

I have   the word **where's**.

Who has   the first card?

Developing Reading Fluency • Gr. 2 © 2003 Creative Teaching Press

Contractions 2 (using 'll and 've)

I have	the first card.
Who has the word	that joins **I will**?

I have	the word **I'll**.
Who has the word	that joins **you have**?

I have	the word **you've**.
Who has the word	that joins **he will**?

I have	the word **he'll**.
Who has the word	that joins **we have**?

I have	the word **we've**.
Who has the word	that joins **you will**?

Developing Reading Fluency • Gr. 2 © 2003 Creative Teaching Press

Read-Arounds

Contractions 2 (using 'll and 've)

I have	the word **you'll**.
Who has the word	that joins **I have**?

I have	the word **I've**.
Who has the word	that joins **they will**?

I have	the word **they'll**.
Who has the word	that joins **they have**?

I have	the word **they've**.
Who has the word	that joins **she will**?

I have	the word **she'll**.
Who has	the first card?

Developing Reading Fluency • Gr. 2 © 2003 Creative Teaching Press

Synonyms

I have   the first card.
Who has the word   that means the same
as **smart**?

I have   the word **clever**.
Who has the word   that means the same
as **quick**?

I have   the word **rapid**.
Who has the word   that means the same
as **hard**?

I have   the word **difficult**.
Who has the word   that means the same
as **small**?

I have   the word **little**.
Who has the word   that means the same
as **strong**?

I have   the word **mighty**.
Who has the word   that means the same
as **late**?

Developing Reading Fluency • Gr. 2 © 2003 Creative Teaching Press

Read-Arounds

Synonyms

I have   the word **tardy**.
Who has the word   that means the same as **nice**?

I have   the word **friendly**.
Who has the word   that means the same as **fragile**?

I have   the word **delicate**.
Who has the word   that means the same as **scary**?

I have   the word **spooky**.
Who has the word   that means the same as **help**?

I have   the word **assist**.
Who has the word   that means the same as **huge**?

I have   the word **enormous**.

Who has   the first card?

Developing Reading Fluency • Gr. 2 © 2003 Creative Teaching Press

Antonyms

I have _____ the first card.
Who has the word _____ that means the opposite of **happy**?

I have _____ the word **angry**.
Who has the word _____ that means the opposite of **empty**?

I have _____ the word **full**.
Who has the word _____ that means the opposite of **brave**?

I have _____ the word **cowardly**.
Who has the word _____ that means the opposite of **exciting**?

I have _____ the word **boring**.
Who has the word _____ that means the opposite of **real**?

I have _____ the word **fake**.
Who has the word _____ that means the opposite of **far**?

Read-Arounds

Antonyms

I have ____ the word **near**.
Who has the word ____ that means the opposite of **warm**?

I have ____ the word **chilly**.
Who has the word ____ that means the opposite of **rough**?

I have ____ the word **smooth**.
Who has the word ____ that means the opposite of **plain**?

I have ____ the word **fancy**.
Who has the word ____ that means the opposite of **rude**?

I have ____ the word **polite**.
Who has the word ____ that means the opposite of **wild**?

I have ____ the word **tame**.

Who has ____ the first card?

Developing Reading Fluency • Gr. 2 © 2003 Creative Teaching Press

Ordinal Numbers

I have   the first card.
Who has the ordinal number
that comes **before third**?

I have   the ordinal number **second**.
Who has the ordinal number
that comes **before sixth**?

I have   the ordinal number **fifth**.
Who has the ordinal number
that comes **after ninth**?

I have   the ordinal number **tenth**.
Who has the ordinal number
that comes **after third**?

I have   the ordinal number **fourth**.
Who has the ordinal number
that comes **after seventh**?

I have   the ordinal number **eighth**.
Who has the ordinal number
that comes **after fourteenth**?

Read-Arounds

Ordinal Numbers

I have the ordinal number **fifteenth**.
Who has the ordinal number
that comes **after tenth**?

I have the ordinal number **eleventh**.
Who has the ordinal number
that comes **after thirteenth**?

I have the ordinal number **fourteenth**.
Who has the ordinal number
that comes **before seventeenth**?

I have the ordinal number **sixteenth**.
Who has the ordinal number
that comes **before seventh**?

I have the ordinal number **sixth**.
Who has the ordinal number
that comes **before twentieth**?

I have the ordinal number **nineteenth**.

Who has the first card?

Developing Reading Fluency • Gr. 2 © 2003 Creative Teaching Press

Place Value and Number Words

I have   the first card.

Who has the number   worth **three tens**?

I have   the number **30**.
Who has the number   worth **two tens and four ones**?

I have   the number **24**.
Who has the number   worth **five tens and two ones**?

I have   the number **52**.
Who has the number   worth **three tens and seven ones**?

I have   the number **37**.
Who has the number   worth **nine tens and nine ones**

I have   the number **99**.
Who has the number   worth **six tens and eight ones**?

Developing Reading Fluency • Gr. 2 © 2003 Creative Teaching Press

Read-Arounds

Place Value and Number Words

I have   the number **68**.
Who has the number   worth **four tens
and six ones**?

I have   the number **46**.
Who has the number   worth **one ten
and eight ones**?

I have   the number **18**.
Who has the number   worth **seven tens
and three ones**?

I have   the number **73**.
Who has the number   worth **nine tens
and zero ones**?

I have   the number **90**.
Who has the number   worth **five tens
and five ones**?

I have   the number **55**.

Who has   the first card?

Developing Reading Fluency • Gr. 2 © 2003 Creative Teaching Press

Plays for Two

Reading is a social event. People who enjoy books like to talk about them and recommend their favorite books. In classrooms, children are often asked to read alone. However, reading with a partner helps children develop phrasing and fluency through repeated oral reading while incorporating the social aspect of reading. Each Plays for Two story is designed for a pair of children to read together. Children will read their parts many times (repeated oral reading strategy) to improve their phrasing and fluency. Then, they will give a final reading for another pair, you, or the whole class. This activity helps reading take on a purpose.

Strategies: repeated oral reading, paired reading

Directions

Materials
- notebook/clear notebook sheet protectors

1. Make two single-sided copies of a paired reading script for each pair of children. (Each script is two pages long.) Do not copy the pages back-to-back. The print bleeds through and is visually distracting to children.
2. Divide the class into pairs. Give each pair a set of scripts.
3. Introduce the text to each pair through guided reading. Then, give partners time to practice reading together. (Have children practice reading and rereading many times to help them develop phrasing and fluency.)
4. To help children develop oral language and public speaking skills in front of a group, invite partners to "perform" their reading in front of the class or for a small group.
5. Train children to give each other specific compliments on their performance. Have them use the words and phrases *sounds like talking, phrasing,* and *fluent*.
6. Store each paired reading script in a clear notebook sheet protector (front to back). Store the sheet protectors in a notebook to make them easily accessible for future use.

Extension
Invite children to make cutouts of the characters and objects in the story to make it more interactive. Have children color the cutouts and glue them to craft sticks to use as props.

The Mystery Box

Genre: mystery

Characters: Friend 1 and Friend 2

Friend 1   Are you ready to play a game? You will get ten chances. You can ask me a question to get a clue. Try to guess what I am hiding in my Mystery Box. Are you ready?

Friend 2   That sounds like fun! I'm ready! Is it alive?

Friend 1   No, it's not alive. Guess again. You have nine more clues.

Friend 2   Is it something I can play with?

Friend 1   That would be fun, but it's not something you can play with.

Friend 2   Is it something I can hold?

Friend 1   Yes, you can hold it if you want to, but you won't want to hold it for very long.

Developing Reading Fluency • Gr. 2 © 2003 Creative Teaching Press

The Mystery Box

Friend 2   Why? Will it burn me?

Friend 1   No! Of course, not! It won't hurt you at all.
Do you have another question?

Friend 2   Is it heavy?

Friend 1   No, it is light. You could hold it on your
finger if you wanted to.

Friend 2   Is it something I could wear?

Friend 1   I don't think you would ever want to wear it,
but it will touch your face.

Friend 2   OH! That was a good clue! It gave me an
idea! Is it something I can eat?

Friend 1   Yes! I'll give you one last clue in a rhyme.
It's round and sweet.
It's a tasty treat.

Friend 2   I know! It's a piece of candy.

Plays for Two

Late for Soccer

Genre: narrative story

Characters: Reader 1 and Reader 2

Reader 1   Hurry up! It's time to go! We are going to be late for soccer!

Reader 2   I'm ready. Let me just get the ball. I was in charge of bringing it to the game this week.

Reader 1   Are you coming?

Reader 2   I can't find the soccer ball anywhere! Have you seen the ball?

Reader 1   The last time I saw the ball was when you were kicking it outside.

Reader 2   That's right! I think it's in the backyard. Let me go see.

Reader 1   Please hurry! We don't want to be late. You know how the coach gets when we're late. He wants us to learn to always be on time.

Developing Reading Fluency • Gr. 2 © 2003 Creative Teaching Press

Late for Soccer

Reader 2   It will just take me a second.

Reader 1   Have you found the soccer ball yet?

Reader 2   I did. I only have one problem. Shiloh found it before me!

Reader 1   Oh, no! Do you mean to tell me that your huge dog has our soccer ball? Well, go get it. We're already late!

Reader 2   Let me go get a bone first. That's the only way he'll ever give us that ball back.

Reader 1   Give him two bones! Let's get going!

Reader 2   It worked! Soccer, here we come!

The Missing Blueberry Pie

Genre: mystery

Characters: Friend 1 and Friend 2

Friend 1 Thanks for asking me to come over after school today.

Friend 2 I'm glad your mom said that you could come to my house to play. Are you hungry? My mom just baked a blueberry pie.

Friend 1 That sounds great! Does she make good pies?

Friend 2 She makes the best pies! Last year her pie won first prize at the county fair. Let's go get some.

Friend 1 Good idea. I'll help set the table with forks and napkins.

Friend 2 Here is a piece for you and a piece for me.

Friend 1 My mom told me to wash my hands before I eat anything. Can I go wash my hands first?

Friend 2 Sure! I have to wash my hands, too.

(Leave. Wash hands. Return.)

Developing Reading Fluency • Gr. 2 © 2003 Creative Teaching Press

The Missing Blueberry Pie

Friend 1   Hey! Half of my pie is gone!

Friend 2   All of my pie is gone! What happened to our blueberry pie?

Friend 1   I don't know. Do you like to do detective work?

Friend 2   Yes! I love to solve mysteries.

Friend 1   Great! Let's start. Who is home? Who could have eaten our pie?

Friend 2   My dad is home right now. He is upstairs working.

Friend 1   Is anyone else home?

Friend 2   My dog is playing outside.

Friend 1   OH, NO! I think I know what happened to our pies!

Friend 2   What do you mean?

Friend 1   Look outside!

Friend 2   BAILEY! What a crazy and MESSY dog!

Plays for Two

The Problem

Genre: narrative story

Characters: Reader 1 and Reader 2

Reader 1   Hi! I have a problem.

Reader 2   Can I help you in any way?

Reader 1   I don't really know. My problem is that I don't know what to collect.

Reader 2   What do you mean?

Reader 1   Well, my sister collects stickers, my brother collects cars, my mom collects teddy bears, and my dad collects stamps.

Reader 2   What do you collect?

Reader 1   That's my problem! I don't know what to collect! Do you have any ideas?

Developing Reading Fluency • Gr. 2 © 2003 Creative Teaching Press

The Problem

Reader 2   Let me think about that for a second. I collect pencils because I like to write. What do you like to do?

Reader 1   I like to read. I can't collect books because they cost too much money. What CAN I collect?

Reader 2   I have the perfect idea! What do you use to keep track of where you leave off when you are reading?

Reader 1   I use a bookmark. OH! What a great idea! I will collect bookmarks.

Reader 2   I have one at home. I'll give it to you to start you off. Before you know it, you will have a bookmark collection!

Plays for Two

Wishes

 Genre: poem

Characters: Friend 1 and Friend 2

Friend 1   Look! There are two shooting stars.

Friend 2   One for you and one for me.

Friend 1   We can make two special wishes

Friend 2   that may come true someday. We'll see.

Friend 1   Let's close our eyes and make a wish.

Friend 2   You can't tell me. I can't tell you.

Friend 1   If we keep it a secret,

Friend 2   one day it might come true.

Friend 1   There is a little secret

Friend 2   that few people really know.

Friend 1   A wish will only be granted

Developing Reading Fluency • Gr. 2 © 2003 Creative Teaching Press

Wishes

Friend 2   if there are kind deeds that you show.

Friend 1   So, if you wish upon a star,

Friend 2   remember to keep one thing in mind.

Friend 1   Your wish will not come true unless

Friend 2   your deeds to others are truly kind.

Friend 1   To get a wish granted for yourself,

Friend 2   you must give something away.

Friend 1   It's not your old clothes or your toys,

Friend 2   it's the kind words that you say!

Friends 1 and 2

If you do what someone else wishes for, your wish will be granted and some more!

Developing Reading Fluency • Gr. 2 © 2003 Creative Teaching Press

An Act of Kindness Goes a Long Way

Genre: news report

Characters: Reporter 1 and Reporter 2

Reporter 1 Hello, all of you in TV land! Do we have big news for you! This story is sure to touch your heart!

Reporter 2 It all began when Tom went on a camp out with his dad and Boy Scout troop.

Reporter 1 While on a hike, Tom and his dad got lost. They were stuck out in the cold air of winter waiting for someone to find them.

Reporter 2 As part of a scout troop, they were always prepared. However, they were cold. Tom wished that he had a warm blanket.

Reporter 1 The troop found them a few hours later. They were safe. They enjoyed the rest of the camping trip.

Reporter 2 Tom kept on thinking about how cold he was. On their drive home, he saw a man on the street who looked cold.

Reporter 1 Guess what Tom did?

Donate Blankets!

Developing Reading Fluency • Gr. 2 © 2003 Creative Teaching Press

An Act of Kindness Goes a Long Way

Reporter 2 He told his dad that he had an idea. His terrific idea is why this story is in the news!

Reporter 1 He is collecting new and used blankets to donate to people who need them for the cold winter.

Reporter 2 Does he need any help?

Reporter 1 He sure does! If any of you out there in TV land would like to help Tom, we're here to tell you how.

Reporter 2 Share the idea with your school. See if you can start a collection box. Maybe some people at your school have blankets they don't need or like anymore.

Reporter 1 Someone out there does need that blanket. Get as many blankets as you can.

Reporter 2 You can drop them off or send them to our news station.

Reporter 1 Many people will be warmer this winter because of your act of kindness. Good luck!

Reporter 2 Wow! What a great thing Tom has started!

The Talent Show

Genre: news report

Characters: Reporter 1 and Reporter 2

Reporter 1 Hello, all of you in TV land! Do we have big news for you!

Reporter 2 We went over to _____ School and saw some amazing talent!

Reporter 1 Yes, _____ School was having their best talent show of the year! You should have seen the incredible singing and dancing!

Reporter 2 Did you see the crowd? Wow! Which act did you enjoy the most?

Reporter 1 I would have to say that the magic act was my favorite. How did he make that penny disappear?

Reporter 2 I have no idea! It must be one of those secrets we will never know. I think my favorite act was the boy who did the bike tricks.

Developing Reading Fluency • Gr. 2 © 2003 Creative Teaching Press

The Talent Show

Reporter 1 That was so scary! It sure takes a great deal of practice to get that good on a bike! Do you think you could do the bike jumps we saw today?

Reporter 2 Are you kidding me? That was amazing! I am lucky I don't fall right off of my bike. I don't know how that boy ever learned to jump over a barrel with his bike.

Reporter 1 I heard that he had a bike trainer who helped him learn about bike safety. I'm sure that helped him learn to do his bike tricks safely.

Reporter 2 I'm glad to hear that. I wonder what kind of talent we will see when we do our news show there next year.

Reporter 1 I'm sure we will be amazed again! Until next year, this is _____ and _____ saying "good night!"

Reporter 2 Thanks for watching CNN—your Classroom News Network!

Plays for Two

The Butterfly and the Frog

Genre: friendship poem (can be read as a limerick)

Characters: Friend 1 and Friend 2

Friend 1   A butterfly flew onto a dog.

Friend 2   A frog hopped onto a log.

Friend 1   The frog said "hi" to the butterfly.

Friend 2   Then the butterfly said "hi" to the dog.

Friend 1   The frog said, "Land on me."

Friend 2   The butterfly was as fast as a bee.

Friend 1   She landed on his back holding a sack.

Friend 2   Then she said, "Would you join me for tea?"

Friend 1   The frog said, "That would be fine."

Friend 2   The butterfly said, "Oh, how divine!"

Developing Reading Fluency • Gr. 2 © 2003 Creative Teaching Press

The Butterfly and the Frog

Friend 1   Then they set up the treats and tea cookie sweets

Friend 2   for the new friends to eat under the pine.

Friend 1   They used good manners to chew

Friend 2   and said "thank you" when they were through.

Friend 1   They cleaned it all up, every single teacup,

Friend 2   then took a nap under the sky so blue.

Friend 1   When it started to get a bit dark

Friend 2   and the sun was only a spark,

Friend 1   they said they would meet another day with new treats.

Friend 2   And the butterfly and frog left the park!

Developing Reading Fluency • Gr. 2 © 2003 Creative Teaching Press

Plays for Two

The Letter

Genre: cumulative tale

Characters: Friend 1 and Friend 2

Friend 1 This is the letter that Brenton wrote.

Friend 2 This is the stamp that went on the letter

Friend 1 that Brenton wrote.

Friend 2 This is the mail carrier

Friend 1 who saw the stamp

Friend 2 that went on the letter that Brenton wrote.

Friend 1 This is the worker at the post office

Friend 2 who got the letter from the mail carrier

Friend 1 who saw the stamp that went on the letter

Friend 2 that Brenton wrote.

Developing Reading Fluency • Gr. 2 © 2003 Creative Teaching Press

The Letter

Friend 1   This is the lady who sorted the mail

Friend 2   that she got from the worker at the post office

Friend 1   who got the letter from the mail carrier

Friend 2   who saw the stamp that went on the letter

Friend 1   that Brenton wrote.

Friend 2   This is the letter!

Friend 1   Guess how we got it!

Friend 2   My dad is the mail carrier who delivered the letter

Friend 1   that Brenton wrote.

Friend 2   Brenton is our cousin!

Friend 1   When we write him a letter back, guess what will happen?

Developing Reading Fluency • Gr. 2 © 2003 Creative Teaching Press

The Farm

Genre: cumulative tale

Characters: Friend 1 and Friend 2

Friend 1	This is the farm.
Friend 2	This is the dairy cow that lives on the farm.
Friend 1	This is the girl who milks the dairy cow
Friend 2	that lives on the farm.
Friend 1	This is the machine that cleans the milk
Friend 2	that was collected by the girl when she milked the dairy cow.
Friend 1	This is the truck that carries the milk
Friend 2	that was cleaned by the machine
Friend 1	that was collected by the girl when she milked the dairy cow.

Developing Reading Fluency • Gr. 2 © 2003 Creative Teaching Press

The Farm

Friend 2   This is the place where the truck goes

Friend 1   to deliver the milk that was cleaned by the machine

Friend 2   that was collected by the girl when she milked the dairy cow.

Friend 1   This is the worker who will package the milk

Friend 2   that came on the truck that delivered the milk

Friend 1   that was cleaned by the machine after it was collected by the girl when she milked the dairy cow.

Friend 2   This is the cow.

Friend 1   She was glad to give us her milk!

Plays for Two

Reader's Theater

Reader's Theater is a motivating and exciting way for children to mature into fluent and expressive readers. Reader's Theater does not use any props, costumes, or materials other than the script, which allows the focus to stay on fluent and expressive reading. The "actors" must tell the story by using only their voices and must rely on their tone of voice, expression, phrasing, and fluency to express the story to the audience. Children are reading for a purpose, which highly motivates them because they take on the roles of characters and bring the characters to life through voice inflection. Each Reader's Theater script is designed for a group of four children. However, the scripts can be modified, if necessary. For example, children can double-up on roles to incorporate paired reading.

Strategies: repeated oral reading model for groups of four, choral reading, paired reading

Materials
- highlighters
- colored file folders
- sentence strips
- yarn

Directions
1. Make four copies of each play. (Each play is several pages long.) Staple together the pages along the left side of the script (not the top). Highlight a different character's part in each script.
2. Gather four folders of the same color for each play. Put one copy of the script in each folder. Write the title of the play and the name of the highlighted character (e.g., The Magic Closet, Arthur) on the front of each folder.
3. Divide the class into groups of four. Give each child in a group a folder of the same color (containing the same script).
4. Have children first read the entire script. (Research supports having children read all of the roles for the first day or two to fully comprehend the story.) Then, have children choose which part they will perform, or assign each child a part. Have children switch folders so that each child has the script with the highlighted character's part that he or she will play.
5. Write each character's name on a sentence strip to make name tags. Hole-punch the name tags, and tie yarn through the holes. Give each child a name tag to wear. Have children spend at least four to five days reading and rereading their part to practice phrasing and fluency.
6. Invite children to perform their play for the whole class, another group, a buddy class, or their parents.

Extension
Invite more advanced readers to choose a script and put on a puppet show with a group. (This type of performance is dramatic play, not Reader's Theater, because children use props with their voices to tell the story.) Invite the group to practice their lines, make puppets (out of paper bags, toilet paper rolls, or craft sticks), and perform the play.

The Soccer Game

Theme: sports

Characters: Coach   Soccer Player 2
               Soccer Player 1   Soccer Player 3

Coach
The big game is today. Are you ready team?

Soccer Players 1, 2, and 3
We're ready!

Soccer Player 1
I practiced at school every day this week, so I'm ready to start the game!

Soccer Player 2
I practiced this week, too! I'm sure I'll kick a goal today!

Coach
Well, you all have the winning attitude! Let's play soccer!

Soccer Player 3
Come on, we can do it! Keep your eye on the net.

Soccer Player 1
Do you remember what the coach told us to do?

Developing Reading Fluency • Gr. 2 © 2003 Creative Teaching Press

Reader's Theater

The Soccer Game

Soccer Player 2
He said that we need to play better defense.

Coach
Come on team! You can do it!

Soccer Player 3
Watch out! Here I come!

Soccer Player 1
Kick it to me! I can kick it in!

Soccer Player 2
Kick it to me and I'll kick it back to you!

Coach
Just kick the ball!

Soccer Player 1
Hooray!

Soccer Player 2
Way to go! That was a great goal!

Soccer Player 3
Good kick! Let's do it again.

Coach
I knew you could do it!

Developing Reading Fluency • Gr. 2 © 2003 Creative Teaching Press

The Day Little Red Riding Hood Met Goldilocks

Themes: fairy tales, friendship

Characters: Narrator 1   Goldilocks
Narrator 2   Little Red Riding Hood

Narrator 1
Now everyone knows the story of Goldilocks and the Three Bears.

Narrator 2
You also know the story of Little Red Riding Hood and the Big Bad Wolf.

Narrator 1
I don't think that wolf was bad. Why are the wolves always bad?

Narrator 2
Let's get on with our story!

Goldilocks
I need to run fast! Those bears are going to chase me! I knew I should not have opened the door of a strange house!

Narrator 1
She should have listened to her mother!

Narrator 2
She was running through the forest. She was on her way home when it started raining.

Reader's Theater

The Day Little Red Riding Hood Met Goldilocks

Goldilocks

Oh, no! It's raining! I don't even have an umbrella! What am I going to do? I'm getting so tired.

Narrator 1

She sat down on a tree trunk to rest.

Goldilocks

I'll just rest here for a minute. Then I'll go straight home.

Narrator 2

Soon, Goldilocks was asleep. Meanwhile, in the northwest corner of the forest, Little Red Riding Hood was leaving her house to carry some bread to her sick grandmother.

Little Red Riding Hood *(singing)*

I'm off to grandma's house, grandma's house, grandma's house. I'm off to grandma's house to cheer her up!

Narrator 1

She was singing and skipping through the forest when it began to rain.

Developing Reading Fluency • Gr. 2 © 2003 Creative Teaching Press

Little Red Riding Hood
It's a good thing I wore my red cloak. I'll just put the hood over my head so I will stay dry. I'm almost there!

Narrator 2
And she sang . . .

Little Red Riding Hood *(singing)*
I'm off to grandma's house, grandma's house, grandma's house. I'm off to grandma's house to cheer her up!

Narrator 1
Just then Goldilocks woke up from her nap. She thought she heard a noise that didn't belong in the forest.

Goldilocks
Hello, is someone out there?

Narrator 2
Little Red Riding Hood nearly jumped out of her boots!

Little Red Riding Hood
Who - who - who's out here in this forest?

Goldilocks
It's me, Goldilocks. Who are you?

Developing Reading Fluency • Gr. 2 © 2003 Creative Teaching Press

Reader's Theater

The Day Little Red Riding Hood Met Goldilocks

Little Red Riding Hood
I'm Little Red Riding Hood. I'm on my way to visit my sick grandma.

Goldilocks
My grandmother is friends with your grandma. Where are you? I'd like to meet you.

Narrator 2
Just then they met face to face.

Little Red Riding Hood
Why are you out here in the woods?

Goldilocks
It's a loooooong story! Can I come with you to your grandma's house?

Little Red Riding Hood
Please join me! It's a bit scary skipping through the forest alone. Tell me how you ended up in the woods.

Narrator 1
The two girls walked together through the forest and shared their stories.

Narrator 2
They became best friends and lived happily ever after.

Developing Reading Fluency • Gr. 2 © 2003 Creative Teaching Press

Two Square Nightmare

Theme: conflict resolution

Characters: Mrs. Sky   Miguel
Trisha   Shanelle

Mrs. Sky

It's recess time boys and girls. Let's get lined up quickly since I have yard duty. We need to be on time.

Miguel

Do you want to play two square with me, Trisha?

Trisha

Sure, that sounds like fun.

Shanelle

You can't play two square with him! You are my friend. You have to play with me. I don't want to play with him.

Trisha

I want to play two square. Do you want to play with Miguel and me?

Shanelle

I don't want to play two square. You're not my friend!

(Shanelle stomps off.)

Reader's Theater

Two Square Nightmare

Trisha
Miguel, can we play something else? Shanelle won't be my friend if I play two square with you.

Miguel
That's silly! Is she your friend or not? Let's go tell Mrs. Sky. It's not fair for Shanelle to say that.

Trisha
Mrs. Sky, Shanelle said that she won't be my friend if I play two square with Miguel.

Mrs. Sky
Did you ask Shanelle if she wanted to play with both of you?

Trisha
Yes and she said I had to play with her because she is my friend.

Mrs. Sky
Is Miguel your friend?

Trisha
Sure!

Developing Reading Fluency • Gr. 2 © 2003 Creative Teaching Press

Two Square Nightmare

Mrs. Sky
What do you want to play, Miguel?

Miguel
I want to play two square and so does Trisha. She is just afraid that Shanelle won't be her friend anymore.

Mrs. Sky
Do you want to have friends who tell you what you can and can't play?

Trisha and Miguel
No way!

Mrs. Sky
Well, that's exactly what you are letting Shanelle do if you decide not to play two square.

Trisha
If we play, do you think she will still be my friend?

Trisha and Miguel *(to audience)*
What should we do?

Reader's Theater

The Magic Closet

Theme: fantasy

Characters: Narrator   Robert
                     Tanya   Arthur

Narrator
Arthur, Tanya, and Robert had a secret. There was a magic closet in their grandma's bedroom. Even their parents didn't know about it!

Robert
I'm so excited we get to go to grandma's house today! Let's get packed right away!

Tanya
Good idea! I'm ready for a new adventure.

Arthur
Shhhh! We have to be very quiet. We don't ever want anyone else to know about the secret closet! We may never get to go in there again.

Robert
Arthur's right! We have to be very careful about when we talk about the magic closet.

Narrator
They got packed and their dad drove them to their grandma's house for the day.

Developing Reading Fluency • Gr. 2 © 2003 Creative Teaching Press

The Magic Closet

Robert, Tanya, and Arthur
Hi, grandma! How are you today?

Narrator
Grandma told them that she was doing fine. She said that she had a surprise for them in the kitchen.

Tanya
Oh, grandma! You baked us your yummy chocolate chip cookies! Thank you!

Narrator
They all sat down to eat cookies with some milk.

Robert and Arthur
Mmmmmm, mmmmm!

Narrator
Grandma told them that she was a bit tired so she was going to take a little nap on the couch.

Robert
Sweet dreams, Grandma!

Arthur
Is anyone ready for an adventure?

The Magic Closet

Robert and Tanya
I am!

Arthur
Let's go!

Narrator
They all went into grandma's room. They opened the closet door.

Arthur
Now be careful! The last person in must leave the door open so we can get back.

Tanya
I'll go last and I won't close the door.

Arthur
Follow me!

Narrator
They walked through the door and into a dark room. Suddenly, they were in a whole new land!

Arthur
We're here! Let's see what is going on in Tiny Land today!

Developing Reading Fluency • Gr. 2 © 2003 Creative Teaching Press

The Magic Closet

Robert
OH! I almost stepped on someone! Hello down there!

Narrator
Tiny people the size of your hand began running to hide.

Tanya
Please don't run away! We are friendly! We came from another land through our grandma's closet.

Narrator
People were peeking out at them from behind toadstools, flowers, and rocks.

Arthur
We want to be your secret friends. We promise not to tell anyone about your land. We love it here!

Robert
We have been here a few times before. We have seen you work in your gardens. You are all so kind to each other. We want to spend time with you.

Reader's Theater

The Magic Closet

Narrator
The people were just about to come out to meet them when . . .

Tanya
I hear Grandma calling us! Hurry!

Arthur
We have to go! We'll be back to meet all of you! We hope to be your friends!

Robert
Hurry! We have to get back through that closet before Grandma finds us missing!

Tanya
Run!

Arthur
I see the closet. Follow me! Come on!

Robert
We're almost there!

Tanya
Hi, Grandma! How was your nap?

Developing Reading Fluency • Gr. 2 © 2003 Creative Teaching Press

Beach Cleanup Day

Theme: character education

Characters: Narrator   Tasha
                     Dotty   Chris

Narrator
Last week, the newspaper reported that more people were needed to help pick up trash along the beach on Saturday. Chris and his sisters are planning to help their parents clean up the beach.

Tasha
Good morning! Sorry I'm late to breakfast! I was getting my backpack ready.

Dotty
That's fine. Dad is out getting the car packed with gloves, shovels, and bags. Mom is in the bedroom getting ready.

Chris
I don't want to go. I'm tired. I want to watch my cartoons and stay home.

Dotty
We all agreed last weekend that since we use the beach it is our job to clean it.

Reader's Theater

Beach Cleanup Day

Chris
But I didn't make the mess on the beach! I always use the trash cans. The trash isn't my problem!

Tasha
Oh, really? Stop to think about what you just said for a second. If everyone felt the same way, then our beaches would look like trash dumps!

Chris
So what?

Dotty
Oh, come on! You know you care about the beaches! Even if you don't ever go to the beach again, you have to think about the crabs and sea creatures. They didn't make the mess!

Tasha
That's right, and they CAN'T clean it up. So . . . it's our job! Get dressed.

Dotty
Mom and Dad said we are all going together, so you don't have a choice anyway.

Developing Reading Fluency • Gr. 2 © 2003 Creative Teaching Press

Beach Cleanup Day

Chris
Fine, I'll go, but I'm not touching any trash!

Narrator
They all rode down to join the rest of the families for the Beach Cleanup Bash.

Chris
Wow! I didn't know there would be so many people! Look! There are some free donuts! Can we get some, Mom?

Narrator
They all got some donuts and began taking their things out of the car.

Dotty
What are we going to do?

Tasha
I saw a list of jobs over by the donuts. Let's go see what we can do to help clean up this beach.

Narrator
They all decided to pick up trash.

Chris
I'm not really going to pick it up. I'm just going with you so I won't be by myself.

Reader's Theater

Beach Cleanup Day

Dotty
No way! Mom!!! Dad!!!

Chris
Fine! I'll pick up a few pieces of trash.

Narrator
They put on their gloves, they picked up their shovels and bags, and EVERYONE began picking up trash.

Tasha
The person with the most trash wins!

Dotty
I'm going to beat all of you! I'm going to pick up the most trash!

Chris
That's what you think! I will win this game! Let's go!

Narrator
At the end of the day, they all looked around at the clean beach.

Chris
You were right. This was our job. It sure was fun. Let's do it again next year!

Developing Reading Fluency • Gr. 2 © 2003 Creative Teaching Press

Making Solar Cookers

Theme: cooperation

Characters: Mr. Arias   Trenton
              Pauli   Megan

Mr. Arias

Well, class, you have met your team. Now you need to figure out which items each person will bring to school. Each team will make a solar cooker to cook nachos. You may now talk about your project.

Trenton

Well, this should be easy and fun!

Pauli

We have three people on our team, and here is our list.

Megan

I'll write a name next to each item we need to bring. Let's see. We need a paper bowl, aluminum foil, and some cheese.

Trenton

Do we need chips?

Pauli

No, Mr. Arias will bring the chips and the black paper.

Developing Reading Fluency • Gr. 2 © 2003 Creative Teaching Press

Making Solar Cookers

Trenton

I'll bring the paper bowl.

Megan

I'll bring the aluminum foil.

Pauli

I'll bring the cheese, but I don't think it's fair.

Megan

Why not?

Pauli

Trenton only has to bring one paper bowl. I have to bring cheese. The cheese costs more than a paper bowl.

Megan

What if we all agree to bring some cheese?

Trenton

That's a good idea! Then we can have really cheesy nachos! So I'll bring a paper bowl and cheese.

(the next day)

Developing Reading Fluency • Gr. 2 © 2003 Creative Teaching Press

Making Solar Cookers

Mr. Arias
Well, class, yesterday you met your team and talked about what you would bring in. Are your teams ready?

Megan
We're ready, but we don't have any aluminum foil. I said I would bring it, but we ran out and my mom didn't want to go to the store last night.

Mr. Arias
Is there a team who will share their aluminum foil with Megan's team?

Megan
Thank you!

Mr. Arias
Let's make solar cookers! You all know what to do. Your main job is to work like a team and help each other. Your reward is some yummy nachos! Have fun!

Pauli
Let's put the chips in first.

Trenton
I think we should line our bowl with aluminum foil first.

Developing Reading Fluency • Gr. 2 © 2003 Creative Teaching Press

Reader's Theater

Making Solar Cookers

Megan

Why?

Trenton

When we make nachos in our oven at home, we put the chips on the foil. I think it helps them get hotter.

Pauli

Does everyone agree? *(Wait.)* Okay, let's wrap the foil over the bowl.

Megan

What should we do with the black paper?

Trenton

My oven is black inside, so let's try making a little box for it.

Pauli

We have to make sure the sun is shining on the cheese, so let's keep the top open.

Megan

Good idea! Wow! What a plan we have. Do you think it will work?

Developing Reading Fluency • Gr. 2 © 2003 Creative Teaching Press

Intervention Instruction

Every section in this book can be used throughout the year to teach, guide, practice, and reinforce reading with phrasing and fluency, which will improve children's reading comprehension. The following activities provide additional practice and instruction for those children who need more help with the strategies that will help them improve their reading fluency. Assess children's stage of fluency development often by referring to the chart on page 7.

Use the following activities with "robotic readers" to help them be successful. The activities in this section will help children focus on the following strategies: phrased reading, automaticity with high-frequency words, recognition of what fluency sounds like at the listening level, and active listening.

Each activity includes an objective, a materials list, and step-by-step directions. The activities are most suited to individualized instruction or very small groups. The activities can be adapted for use with larger groups or a whole-class setting in some cases.

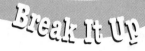

Strategy: explicit phrasing

Objectives: Each child will identify where the natural language phrases are in text. Each child will visually recognize that phrases are usually two to four words (chunks) spoken together.

Materials
- paragraph from student writing, anthology, or story
- thin markers

Directions

1. Make a copy of a paragraph of readable text. It must be at children's easy reading level so that no decoding is required.

2. Model and guide children through the first few sentences.

3. Read each sentence. Then, reread each sentence, and use a thin marker to draw arc-shaped lines from the first word to the last word in the phrased chunks as you read. Continue this through all of the sentences. (In most second-grade texts, you will have between two to four phrases in each sentence.)

4. Discuss with children what they notice about each phrase. Tell them that you will reread each sentence while they focus on the phrases you marked.

5. Tell children to draw arc-shaped lines to identify phrases in the sentences in the rest of the paragraph.

6. As each child finishes, ask him or her to read to you. Encourage children to focus on the marked phrases as they read. Invite children to discuss what they learned and what they will do when they read a book (in which lines cannot be drawn).

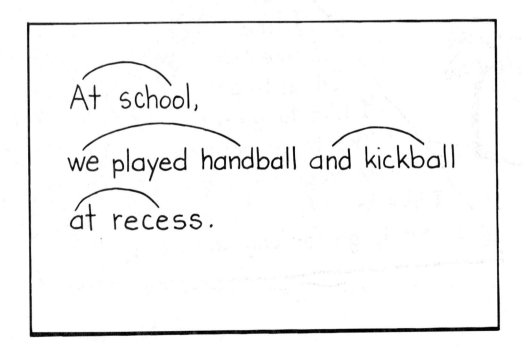

Phrasing Pyramids

Strategy: explicit phrasing

Objective: Each child will practice reading phrases of increasing length with fluency.

Materials
- Pyramids reproducible (page 90)

Directions

1. Give each child a Pyramids reproducible.

2. Discuss the sample in the first pyramid. Model how to read each line of increasing length as one continuous phrase. (Option: Use guided practice following the Fantastic Five Format described on page 8.)

3. Brainstorm topics that children can write about to create sentences for the blank pyramids.

4. Have each child write a sentence in one of the blank pyramids (using the same format as the example).

5. Read aloud each child-written pyramid to further model phrasing to the group.

6. Invite children to switch papers with a classmate and read each other's sentences.

7. Have children write a sentence in the second blank pyramid and then switch papers and read each other's sentences.

8. Invite children to discuss what they learned by completing this activity.

Intervention Instruction

Pyramids

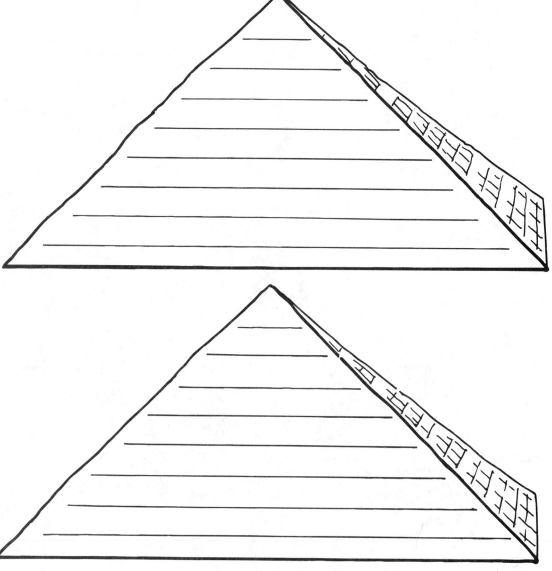

I
I like
I like to
I like to go
I like to go to
I like to go to the
I like to go to the pet
I like to go to the pet store.

90

Phrasing Fun with Friends

Strategy: explicit phrasing

Objectives: Each child will understand what phrasing sounds like and looks like in text. Each child will transfer phrasing and fluency to ongoing text.

Materials

- A Day at the Carnival 1 and 2 reproducibles (pages 92–93)
- Grocery Shopping 1 and 2 reproducibles (pages 94–95)
- familiar children's books

Directions

1. Copy a class set of the A Day at the Carnival 1 and 2 reproducibles.
2. Divide the class into small groups. Write in each blank the name of a child in the group you are working with.
3. Give each child the A Day at the Carnival 1 reproducible. Read the text following the Fantastic Five Format (described on page 8).

> **Step 1:** Model how to read each phrase.
> **Step 2:** Echo reading—Read one phrase at a time as children repeat.
> **Step 3:** Choral reading—Guide children as they read with phrasing.
> **Step 4:** Independent reading—Have children read the phrases without you.
> **Step 5:** Reverse echo reading—Have children read the phrases, and then repeat them.

4. Give each child the A Day at the Carnival 2 reproducible. (It has the same phrases as reproducible 1, but it is written in an ongoing text format and has an additional paragraph of related text. This reproducible is the KEY! It is very important that you do not skip this reproducible because children will practice transferring their skills of reading phrases fluently to reading sentences in a paragraph fluently.)
5. Choral read the reproducible together. Then, invite the group to read it aloud to you.
6. Repeat the activity with the Grocery Shopping reproducibles for further practice.
7. Invite children to practice their phrasing and fluency by reading a familiar book. Easy guided reading books are perfect.

Intervention Instruction

A Day at the Carnival 1

_____ and _____

went to the carnival.

They were hungry

so they

ate a snack first.

Then they went

on a roller coaster.

They went

on scary rides,

fast rides,

and funny rides.

They had fun

at the carnival!

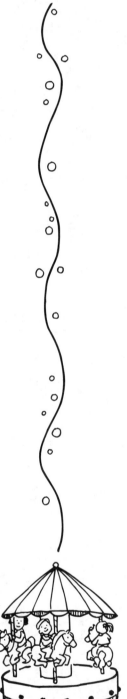

Developing Reading Fluency • Gr. 2 © 2003 Creative Teaching Press

A Day at the Carnival 2

_____ and _____ went to the carnival. They were hungry so they ate a snack first. Then they went on a roller coaster. They went on scary rides, fast rides, and funny rides. They had fun at the carnival!

On their way home, they talked about how much fun they had. They both agreed that the roller coaster was the most fun!

Developing Reading Fluency • Gr. 2 © 2003 Creative Teaching Press

Grocery Shopping 1

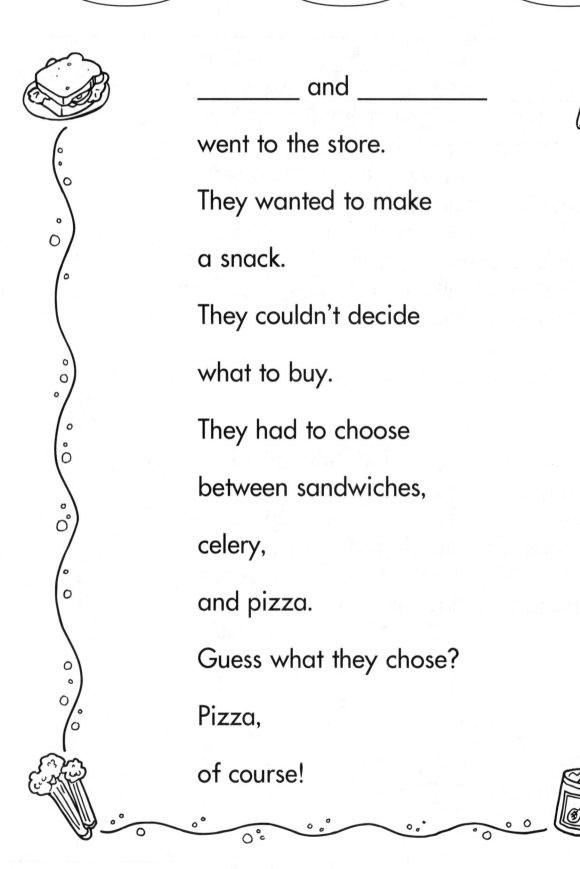

_____ and _____

went to the store.

They wanted to make

a snack.

They couldn't decide

what to buy.

They had to choose

between sandwiches,

celery,

and pizza.

Guess what they chose?

Pizza,

of course!

Developing Reading Fluency • Gr. 2 © 2003 Creative Teaching Press

Grocery Shopping 2

_____ and _____ went to the store.

They wanted to make a snack. They

couldn't decide what to buy. They had to

choose between sandwiches,

celery, and pizza. Guess what they

chose? Pizza, of course!

They bought English muffins, cheese, and

sauce. They made little faces on

the pizza. Have you ever tried that?

Intervention Instruction

Strategy: explicit phrasing

Objectives: Each child will understand why punctuation is so important. Each child will identify punctuation in text that is read aloud and apply this in reading and writing.

Materials
- scissors
- small index cards
- short stories or books

Directions

1. Cut small index cards in half. Give each child four cut cards.
2. Tell children to draw a period, a question mark, an exclamation point, and quotation marks on separate cards.
3. Read aloud a short story. Tell children to hold up a card to indicate the type of punctuation needed in the sentence. For example, as you change speaking voices for different characters, they will hold up the quotation marks. If you ask a question, they will hold up a question mark.
4. Explain to children that good stories have sentences that use different kinds of punctuation. They are not all simple sentences or statements.
5. Invite children to work with a partner. Have pairs take turns reading a short story or book to each other. Tell the listener to hold up the index card that indicates what punctuation he or she hears at the end of each sentence. Then, invite partners to switch roles.
6. Remind children that good readers and writers pay close attention to the punctuation clues. Encourage them to do this when they read and write.